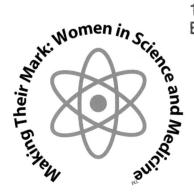

Making Their Mark: Women in Science and Medicine™

Marie Curie
Nobel Prize-Winning Physicist

Liza N. Burby

The Rosen Publishing Group's
PowerKids Press™
New York

Published in 1997 by The Rosen Publishing Group, Inc.
29 East 21st Street, New York, NY 10010

First Edition

Book Design: Erin McKenna

Photo Credits: p. 4 © Corbis-Bettman; p. 7 © Underwood & Underwood/Corbis-Bettman; p. 8 © Corbis-Bettman; pp. 11, 12, 15, 16, 19 © Corbis-Bettman; p. 20 © H. Armstrong Roberts Inc.

Burby, Liza N.
    Marie Curie / Liza N. Burby.
        p.   cm. — (Making their mark)
    Includes index.
    Summary: Discusses the life of Marie Curie, whose work in physics helped to change the world.
    ISBN 0-8239-5024-7 (library bound)
    1. Curie, Marie, 1867–1934—Juvenile literature. 2. Chemists—Poland—Biography—Juvenile literature.
[1. Curie, Marie, 1867–1934. 2. Scientists. 3. Women—Biography.] I. Title. II. Series: Burby, Liza N.
Making their mark.
    QD22.C8B87 1996
    540' .92—dc20
                                      96-41734
                                        CIP
                                        AC

Manufactured in the United States of America

Contents

1	A Love for Learning	5
2	A Hard Time in Poland	6
3	Dreams of the Future	9
4	Studying Physics and Math	10
5	Marie and Pierre Get Married	13
6	Marie Wants to Learn More	14
7	An Exciting Discovery	17
8	The Nobel Prize	18
9	Marie Carries on Alone	21
10	Changing the World	22
	Glossary	23
	Index	24

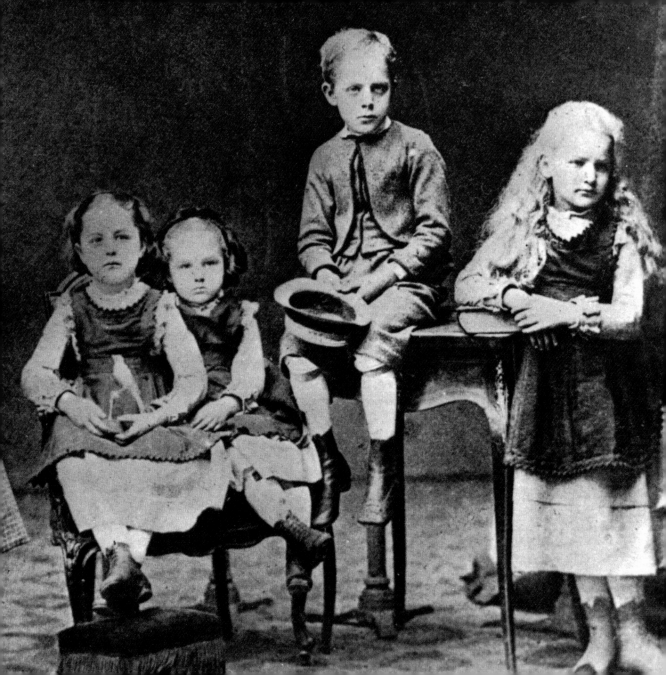

A Love for Learning

Marie Curie was born Marya Sklodowska in Warsaw, Poland, on November 7, 1867. Both of Marya's parents were teachers. Her father taught **physics** (FIZZ-iks) and math, and her mother taught music. They also taught their children to love learning. Marya began reading books when she was just four years old. Learning was so important to Marya, she often forgot to eat, sleep, or even go outside.

◄ All of the Sklodowska children were taught that learning is important.

A Hard Time in Poland

Life was not easy in Poland. A country called Russia ruled the area where Marya's family lived. The Russians did not allow the Polish people to speak their own **language** (LANG-widge). Teachers who were caught teaching Polish to their students could be punished. But Marya's father loved his country and his language. At night, he read Polish stories to his children. Marya learned Russian, but she also knew the Polish language.

Warsaw was ruled by Russia when Marya and her family lived there. ▶

Dreams of the Future

Marya loved all subjects, but physics and **chemistry** (KEM-iss-tree) excited her most of all. As a little girl, she loved to look at her father's physics **equipment** (ee-KWIP-ment). As a young woman, she decided she wanted to spend her life working in physics. She would have to study at a **university** (yoo-nih-VER-sih-tee). The University of Poland did not allow women as students. But a university in Paris, France, did. Marya worked to earn enough money to go there.

◀ Marya looked forward to learning new things at the Sorbonne, a university in Paris.

9

Studying Physics and Math

In 1891, when Marya was 23 years old, she went to Paris. She changed her name to Marie, which was the French way to spell her name. In Paris, Marie could study anything she liked and speak any language she wanted. She wanted to study physics and math. Two years later, she became the first woman in the world to get a **degree** (dih-GREE) in physics. The next year she got a degree in math.

Marie graduated from the Sorbonne, a university in Paris, with degrees in physics and math. ▶

Marie and Pierre Get Married

In 1894, Marie met a young **scientist** (SY-en-tist) in Paris. His name was Pierre Curie. Soon they fell in love. They were married in 1895. Pierre worked as a teacher at the School of Physics and Chemistry. He did not make much money. But the Curies did not mind. Like Marie, Pierre loved science and learning more than money.

◀ At first Pierre was surprised that Marie was interested in science.

13

Marie Wants to Learn More

After her daughter, Irene, was born, Marie decided she wanted to be a physics teacher. To do this, she had to write a paper about something new in physics. She was curious about a discovery by the scientist Henri Becquerel. Becquerel learned that an **element** (EL-eh-ment) called **uranium** (yoo-RAY-nee-um) made **rays** (RAYZ) that gave light. Marie wanted to know if other elements did this. Now she knew what she wanted to write about.

Marie set out to discover more about other elements. ▶

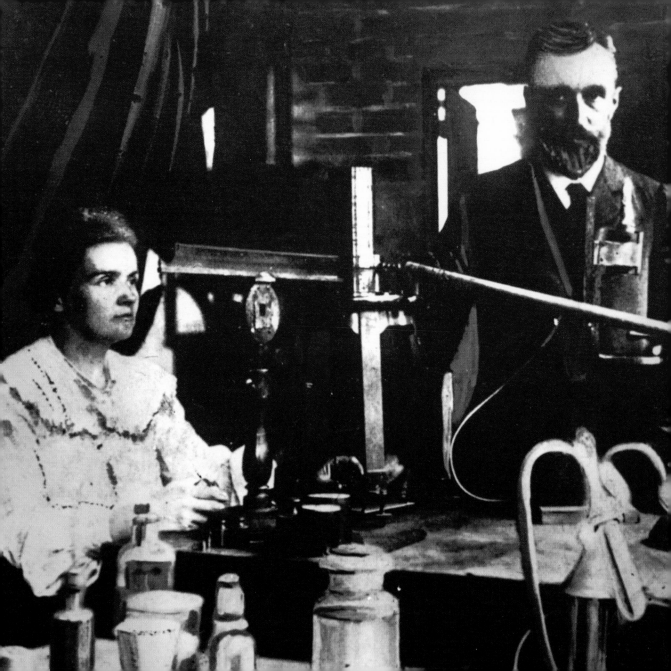

An Exciting Discovery

Marie discovered that uranium was made of other elements that no one knew about. Other scientists were excited to hear that there might be more elements in uranium. Marie set out to find them. Pierre helped. In July 1898, they discovered an element that Marie named **polonium** (pe-LOH-nee-um). This element was named after Poland. In December, they discovered their second element, **radium** (RAY-dee-um).

◀ Pierre and Marie discovered two new elements while working together.

17

The Nobel Prize

The Curies also learned that radium had a new kind of **energy** (EN-er-jee) that Marie called **radioactivity** (RAY-dee-oh-ak-TIV-ih-tee). This is the name she gave to explain how the new element's rays moved. These discoveries were very important. They helped other scientists learn about ways to use radium. For their work, the Curies were given the Nobel Prize in 1903. This is the highest award for a scientist. Marie was the first woman to win it.

Marie Curie was the first woman in history to receive a Nobel Prize. ▶

18

Marie Carries on Alone

In 1904, their second daughter, Eve, was born. Pierre died in an accident two years later. Marie was sad for a long time. But she continued the work they had once done together. She also became a physics teacher. In 1911, she won a second Nobel Prize. This award was for her work in chemistry. No one had ever won two of these awards before. In 1915, her daughter, Irene, began to work with Marie. Irene would one day win a Nobel Prize, too.

◄ Irene, Marie's daughter, worked with Marie in physics.

21

Changing the World

Marie **dedicated** (DED-ih-KAY-ted) her life to science. But her work with radium had made her sick. She did not know that it is a deadly poison. Marie died in 1934, when she was 66 years old. During her life, Marie had made important discoveries. Her work would lead to a medicine for **cancer** (CAN-ser) and new ways to create energy. Marie's love of learning and her dream of working with physics helped to change the world and to open doors for women in science.

Glossary

cancer (CAN-ser) A harmful sickness.

chemistry (KEM-iss-tree) The study of what things are made of.

dedicated (DED-ih-kay-ted) To work hard for something.

degree (dih-GREE) An award given when someone finishes school.

element (EL-eh-ment) One of over 100 substances from which all other things are made.

energy (EN-er-jee) A force in nature and in humans that makes activity.

equipment (ee-KWIP-ment) Tools or supplies a person uses to do something.

language (LANG-widge) The words people use to speak.

physics (FIZZ-iks) The study of how to make things move.

polonium (pe-LOH-nee-um) A radioactive element.

radioactivity (RAY-dee-oh-ak-TIV-ih-tee) The energy that is given off from tiny parts of some elements.

radium (RAY-dee-um) A radioactive element sometimes used to help people with cancer.

rays (RAYZ) Very strong light beams.

scientist (SY-en-tist) A person who studies the way things are and act in the universe.

university (yoo-nih-VER-sih-tee) A large school that students go to after high school.

uranium (yoo-RAY-nee-um) An element.

Index

B
Becquerel, Henri, 14

C
cancer, 22
chemistry, 9, 21
Curie, Eve, 21
Curie, Irene, 14, 21
Curie, Pierre, 13, 17, 18, 21

E
elements, 14, 17, 18
energy, 18, 22

M
math, 5, 10

N
Nobel Prize, 18, 21

P
physics, 5, 9, 10, 14, 21, 22
polonium, 17

R
radioactivity, 18
radium, 17, 18, 22
rays, 14, 18

S
School of Physics and Chemistry, 13
science, 13, 22
scientist, 13, 14, 17, 18

U
uranium, 14, 17